The Fourth Estate

Journalism in
North America

The Muckrakers and Progressive Reformers

Jacqueline Conciatore Senter

Cavendish
Square

New York

Published in 2019 by Cavendish Square Publishing, LLC
243 5th Avenue, Suite 136, New York, NY 10016

Copyright © 2019 by Cavendish Square Publishing, LLC

First Edition

Website: cavendishsq.com

This publication represents the opinions and views of the author based on his or her personal experience, knowledge, and research. The information in this book serves as a general guide only. The author and publisher have used their best efforts in preparing this book and disclaim liability rising directly or indirectly from the use and application of this book.

All websites were available and accurate when this book was sent to press.

Cataloging-in-Publication Data

Names: Senter, Jacqueline Conciatore.
Title: The muckrakers and progressive reformers / Jacqueline Conciatore Senter.
Description: New York : Cavendish Square, 2019. | Series: The fourth estate: journalism in North America | Includes glossary and index.
Identifiers: ISBN 9781502634771 (pbk.) | ISBN 9781502634757 (library bound) | ISBN 9781502634788 (6pack) | ISBN 9781502634764 (ebook)
Subjects: LCSH: Journalism--Social aspects--United States--History--20th century. | Social problems--Press coverage--United States. | Progressivism (United States politics)--History--20th century.
Classification: LCC PN4888.S6 S47 2019 | DDC 302.230973'09042--dc23

Editorial Director: David McNamara
Editor: Caitlyn Miller
Copy Editor: Nathan Heidelberger
Associate Art Director: Amy Greenan
Designer: Christina Shults
Production Coordinator: Karol Szymczuk
Photo Research: J8 Media

The photographs in this book are used by permission and through the courtesy of: Cover, p 8-9 Jacob Riis/Bettmann/Getty Images; p. 2 (and throughout the book) StillFX/Shutterstock.com; p. 4, 45 Hulton Archive/Getty Images; p. 12-13, 26-28, 31, 35, 43 Everett Historical/Shutterstock.com; p. 15 Library of Congress/Wikimedia Commons/File:Triangle Shirtwaist coffins.jpg/Public Domain; p. 20, 48, 65 Bettmann/Getty Images; p. 22 The Archives/Alamy Stock Photo; p. 40, 73, 95 Library of Congress; p. 53 Transcendental Graphics/Getty Images; p. 55, 86 Universal History Archive/Getty Images; p. 57 Everett Collection/Alamy Stock Photo; p. 60 MPI/Getty Images; p. 74-75 North Wind Picture Archives; p. 76 The Print Collector/Getty Images; p. 81 Kimberly Butler/The LIFE Images Collection/Getty Images; p. 88-89 Ken Feil/The Washington Post/Getty Images; p. 92 Neftali/Shutterstock.com; p. 93 Screenshot; p. 96-97 Saul Loeb/AFP/Getty Images.

Printed in the United States of America

CONTENTS

The Fourth Estate

Journalism in North America

By 1900, when this photo of Broadway in New York City was taken, nearly half of all Americans lived in cities. Rapid growth led to hardships, including overcrowded tenements and disease.

The Gilded Age

The muckraking journalists were born out of widespread change in American society during the latter part of the nineteenth century. Industrialization and urbanization had changed America's landscape, habits, and sense of what was possible. It was now the age of big business. The first transcontinental railroads and the telegraph had created opportunities for businesses to grow as never before. People, products, and natural resources such as coal and timber could move across the country in days rather than months. Likewise, communication could be almost instantaneous, making business transactions much more efficient.

It was also the age of the "robber baron"—the name given to big-business leaders including oil magnate John D. Rockefeller, banker J. P. Morgan, and railway tycoon Cornelius Vanderbilt. (Others prefer to call them "captains of industry.") These men succeeded in building industrial-age empires and amassing tremendous wealth because they had a grand vision, driving ambition, and, in the minds of some, plenty of greed. Many of the robber barons had opulent lifestyles, with "palaces" in exclusive neighborhoods like San Francisco's Nob Hill and mansions by the sea called "cottages."

Mark Twain coined a term for the times: the Gilded Age. (To be "gilded" means to be coated in a thin layer of gold.) Beneath the glittering surface—looking past the fine clothes, furs, palatial homes, and extravagances such as gold-trimmed personal railroad cars—Twain suggested, lay corruption and other societal ills.

Impoverished people, especially from Europe, set their sights on America, the land of opportunity, where the streets were supposed to be paved in gold. Fourteen million brave immigrants traveled to America between 1860 and 1900 by crossing the ocean. Many settled in cities, especially in New York. Likewise, rural dwellers shifted from the country to cities.

By the turn of the century, roughly 40 percent of all Americans lived in cities. With these new city dwellers came urban development. Big apartment buildings known as tenements went up and filled up. Mass transit grew. Trolleys, cable cars, and subways were built to move all the people from home to work.

"Appalling Misery"

The age was full of promise. But the rapid industrialization, immigration, and urbanization also produced terrible ills: poverty and disease; harsh, dangerous working conditions for workers, many of whom were children; dark, overcrowded tenements.

Poverty tarnished the glow of the Gilded Age and became a focus of the muckraking journalists, who helped shape the reform era that followed the Gilded Age. "The wealthy class is becoming more wealthy; but the poorer class is becoming more dependent," said journalist and economist Henry George in his 1879 book *Progress and Poverty*. "The gulf between the employed and the employer is growing wider; social contrasts are becoming sharper; as liveried carriages appear, so do barefooted children ... Beggars are becoming so common that where it was once thought a crime little short of highway robbery to refuse food to one who asked for it, the gate is now barred and the bulldog loosed."

Especially in tenement neighborhoods, people didn't have to look far for evidence of this shadow side of the industrial boom. "There was appalling misery in New York," says historian David McCullough. "Terrible crowding. Terrible slums. All kinds of disease. Crime, prostitution. Children sleeping in the streets, children begging in the streets. It was crowded. It was dirty. It smelled terrible, much of it. And traffic was worse than it is today, if that's possible to imagine."

There was a sizable number of people in society back then who believed poverty was a sign of personal failings rather than unequal social conditions. An example is Baptist minister and philanthropist Russell Conwell, who traveled around the country giving lectures about how to get rich. In his lecture *Acres of Diamonds*, he said:

> The number of poor who are to be sympathized with is very small. To sympathize with a man whom God has punished for his sins ... is to do wrong ... Let us remember there is not a poor person in the United States who was not made poor by his own shortcomings, or by the shortcomings of some one else. It is all wrong to be poor, anyhow.

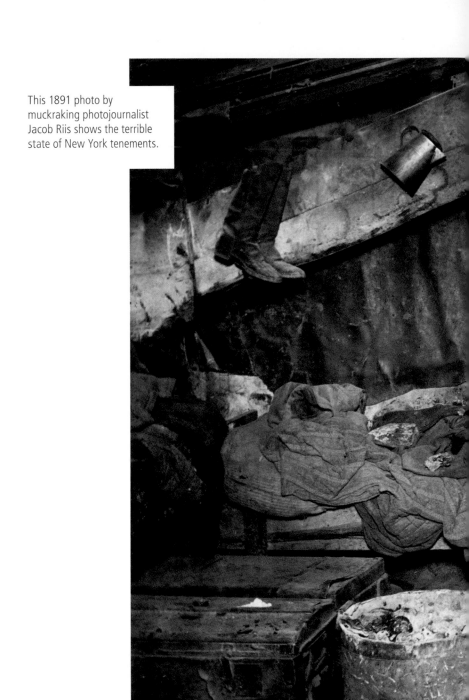

This 1891 photo by muckraking photojournalist Jacob Riis shows the terrible state of New York tenements.

Such beliefs were fueled by a philosophy at the time tied to nineteenth-century scientist Charles Darwin's theories about the evolution of species in the natural world. People transferred Darwin's ideas about the survival of the fittest to human society. Believing in social Darwinism allowed people to justify the enormous gap between rich and poor and to dismiss the needs and plight of the poor.

A group of smart and passionate journalists—the muckrakers—were to play a very big role in changing these attitudes toward poverty and shining a light on the social injustices contributing to the growing number of poor.

Monopolies Become a Problem

Most leaders of the day believed government should take a hands-off approach when it came to business, a doctrine known as laissez-faire economics. This "let it be" approach allowed industry bosses to use unethical methods to squeeze out competitors and establish monopolies.

A monopoly exists when one company owns or controls an entire industry, such as steel or oil. A monopoly can set unreasonable prices, make inferior products, give poor service, and dismiss the customer's needs because it has no competition. Therefore, the customer has no other choices. The company becomes all-powerful—able, for example, to influence lawmakers in its own interests. It also can put smaller, local, or family-run companies out of business.

As a child, journalist Ida Tarbell saw her father's business suffer under the shadow of John D. Rockefeller's boot. Rockefeller's company, Standard Oil, shut out most of Cleveland's oil refiners by gaining market advantages and forcing the owners of the smaller companies to sell their businesses to Standard or be run out of business. Over a period of three to four months, Standard Oil purchased twenty-two of the twenty-six oil refiners around Cleveland, paying the former owners with stock in Standard Oil. Today, Standard's takeover of the local oil market is known as the "Cleveland Massacre." Tarbell's father never fully recovered, financially or emotionally, from his struggle against Rockefeller's monopoly. Her family's story is but one example of the issues muckrakers would take on in print.

Political Machines and Party Bosses

The Gilded Age was marked by a great deal of corruption in government as well as business. In the cities, tough, politically savvy men known as party bosses used shady tactics and backdoor dealings to accumulate wealth, power, and influence. They were the power behind the curtain of city life and politics. Although their party "machines" sometimes took care of the needs of the poor and immigrants better than government did, that wasn't saying much. In the end, they were more interested in serving their own interests than the people's interests. One of the most infamous party machines was New York's Tammany Hall. It was run for a long time by the famous Boss Tweed. Tweed was brought down in part by the efforts of a different kind of muckraker: a political cartoonist.

Reformers

Many Americans felt the country had to adjust course. Especially after the turn of the century, people wanted reforms that would end corruption, curb big business, and stop exploitation of the working class. The period from roughly the 1890s until the 1920s is known as the Progressive Era. Those who fought for change were known as progressive reformers.

The reformers included politicians, writers, labor leaders, women interested in suffrage (giving women the right to vote), and other groups. They weren't always united. But they all had faith that society could improve and that government, pushed by the people, could—and should—make life better for the people.

The progressive reform movement was aided greatly by the journalists later known as muckrakers. President Theodore Roosevelt, a reformer himself, coined this name because the muckrakers turned up the mud and filth—the "muck"—of society. Some of the journalists didn't like this label and might have preferred to describe themselves as investigative writers who exposed terrible societal problems government wasn't doing much about.

Societal changes at the turn of the century were preceded by innovations including the steam press, telegraph, locomotive, and steamboat, all shown in this colorized 1876 lithograph.

The Triangle Shirtwaist Factory Fire

Many of the social and labor problems muckraking journalists exposed were matters of life and death. No event illustrates this more clearly than the Triangle Shirtwaist Factory fire of 1911. The tragedy occurred as garment workers in New York City, including the mostly young and female Triangle workers, had been demanding better treatment. They wanted to earn more than $6 a week (about $150 in 2018), to work less than twelve to fourteen hours a day, and to have reasonable working conditions. They were made, for example, to work quickly, and they were sometimes even denied bathroom breaks. Their pay was already low, but they had to pay for needles and thread and were docked for errors, which meant the companies took money out of their paychecks when they made sewing mistakes.

Although four small fires had already broken out in the Asch Building where the factory was located, the building owners insisted the structure was safe. Toward 5:00 p.m. on Saturday, March 25, 1911, a fire broke out again, on the eighth floor. This one spread quickly, lapping up the factory's fabric pieces and pattern tissue paper. Although many got out, the workers on the ninth floor were trapped. With no way to escape the flames, many of the women jumped from the ninth-floor windows facing the street to their deaths. Horrified onlookers would never forget the sight or sound of the bodies hitting pavement. When the last person came out, a total of 90 people had jumped to their deaths. Including those who died inside, the total death toll was 146.

New York and the entire country were horrified by the factory fire, which highlighted the hardships facing young

Officials stand beside coffins holding victims of the Triangle Shirtwaist Factory fire.

immigrant women in New York. The grief the nation's middle and upper classes may have felt did not keep the building owners from being acquitted at trial, however. Max Blanck and Isaac Harris were exonerated even though they had failed to put in sprinklers, have fire drills, or put adequate fire escapes outside the Asch Building. Writing about the fire, the progressive magazine *La Follette's* quoted a fire marshal: "So far as I can discover there never has been a fire drill in the factory. In my opinion it would take seven hundred girls three hours to reach the street by the one fire escape. Nine-tenths of the employees cannot speak English, yet I could not find a sign in Yiddish or Italian pointing out the fire exits."

Witnesses also stated at the trial that the women couldn't escape the ninth floor because the doors had been locked. There are differing explanations as to why. Some say they were locked to keep out labor union organizers. Others say it was part of the system the factory used to check for theft of fabric or to make sure no worker sneaked out.

In the end, the loss of life was not completely in vain. Thanks in part to news coverage of the terrible tragedy, the Triangle fire led to reforms such as workplace safety laws that improved life for workers in New York and around the country.

Penny Papers

The muckrakers were part of the golden age of journalism, which began with the advent of penny papers in the 1830s. Steam-powered printing presses made penny papers possible. They could print thousands of pages in an hour, whereas the earlier hand-operated presses could print only hundreds.

The penny paper—which cost one cent—revolutionized journalism. Suddenly, more people could buy newspapers. Previously, a single paper cost about six cents, which was simply more than many people could afford. In addition to technological changes, the penny papers were able to sell at such a low price because they relied on money from the sale of ad space.

With the price cut, publishers clearly intended to reach more "regular" people. In fact, the motto of the first penny paper in New York, the *Sun*, was: "It Shines for All." And the publishers made it as convenient as possible for people to get papers, using newsboys to hawk papers on the street.

The penny papers ran what is known as "sensational" news, or news that causes a sensation by focusing on dramatic, exotic, or gossip-worthy topics. These topics included crime, love scandals, and stories about the unusual. In their pursuit of the sensational, the penny papers sometimes bent the truth. Or made it up. In 1835, for example, the *Sun* published a series of six articles claiming scientists had discovered a civilization on the moon occupied by humanoids with bat wings, blue unicorns, beavers without tails, and more. Readers overall weren't upset at the "Great Moon Hoax." Many found it funny. The penny papers also widened their reader base by being more politically independent than previous newspapers, which had been mouthpieces for political parties.

Personal Journalism

Beginning around the 1840s, journalism entered a phase known as "personal journalism." During this period, several big-city newspapers reflected the personalities and opinions of their editors. The papers' editorials—that is, articles that lay out arguments and opinion as opposed to reporting solely facts and news—were important to these papers and their readers. The editorials were widely read and discussed, and they influenced public opinion.

The editors pushed for reform in the public interest. *New York Tribune* editor Horace Greeley, for example, used his pages to argue for an end to slavery and better conditions for workers.

Yellow Journalism

The yellow journalism of the nineteenth century featured sensational news designed to boost circulation (the number of people who subscribe to or buy a paper). This period centers around the infamous circulation wars between two big New York publishers, Joseph Pulitzer (*New York World*) and William Randolph Hearst (*New York Journal*). Vying for the same readers, the papers exaggerated news to make it more sensational, featured big exclamatory headlines, and never found a murder they didn't write up.

This period peaked with events surrounding the Spanish-American War. When the US battleship the USS *Maine* was destroyed in Cuba's Havana Harbor, killing more than 260 men, the *World* and *Journal* covered the tragedy in angry tones. Although it wasn't clear if the *Maine* had been attacked or if the blast had been an accident, the papers stirred up a desire for revenge.

Historians disagree about the influence of news coverage leading up to the war. But the American public seemed to believe the brutal Spanish regime in Cuba was responsible for the bombing. "Remember the *Maine*. To hell with Spain!" became a popular rallying cry.

One legend from these days illustrates the outsize persona Hearst achieved. When newspaper artist Frederic Remington went to Cuba to draw scenes from the expected revolution there, Remington cabled Hearst that, in fact, there would be no war. Hearst supposedly cabled back: "You furnish the pictures. I'll furnish the war." (Historians have found no evidence that such a cable was actually sent.)

Even the style of journalism was named after the influence of Pulitzer and Hearst. Most say the term "yellow journalism" derived from a popular cartoon character that appeared in both papers, the "Yellow Kid," drawn by Richard F. Outcault. Outcault worked first at Pulitzer's paper and then at Hearst's.

The Muckraking Movement Takes Off

The practice of exposing government and other leaders' misdeeds through writing goes back a long way—at least to the gifted ancient Roman politician and speechmaker Cicero, says muckraker expert David Mark Chalmers. Likewise, muckraking journalist Lincoln Steffens said, "I was not the original muckraker. The prophets of the Old Testament were ahead of me."

If the techniques and motives were not new, what was new at the time of the muckrakers was their access to a mass audience and the spirit of reform. This spirit led the nation to consider and then accept a more active role for government, especially when it came to protecting the interests of people through laws and policies.

A comprehensive picture of the movement involves the muckrakers' own life stories and, most important, the stories they wrote. Danish immigrant Jacob Riis set the stage for the muckrakers in New York City by not only writing about horrible living conditions but also using recent technology to take photos that depicted the harsh realities of urban poverty. Riis came to the United States as so many had before and would after—a penniless immigrant. But through a combination of writing talent, compassion, dedication, and cleverness, he became a leading photojournalist, a public figure, and even a friend to President Theodore Roosevelt. In the southern states, the courageous Ida B. Wells drew the world's attention to issues of racial injustice, especially the evil of lynching.

Riis and Wells wrote in the 1890s, but it was not until after the turn of the century that the muckraking movement fully emerged. Three journalists were at the heart of the action: Ida Tarbell, Ray Stannard Baker, and Lincoln Steffens. The leading muckraking magazine, McClure's, published many of their stories. This influential journal was founded by S. S. McClure, a creative genius and visionary publisher. As we read about these journalists and their lives, we'll also explore their reporting techniques. In addition, we'll hear about a few writers whose muckraking took a more literary form—Upton Sinclair most famously, and a poet or two as well. Lastly, we'll discuss the tools reform journalists used to get their stories and make them powerful and unique.

Harriet Beecher Stowe

In 1850, the US Congress passed the Fugitive Slave Act, which empowered appointed officials called commissioners to send escaped slaves back to their former captors. Citizens who didn't cooperate with the law—even Northern abolitionists—faced stiff penalties.

Isabella Jones Beecher wrote to her sister-in-law about the law: "If I could use a pen as you can, Hatty, I would write something that would make this whole nation feel what an accursed thing slavery is." Harriet Beecher Stowe was moved by Isabella's words. "I will write something," she vowed to her family. "I will if I live."

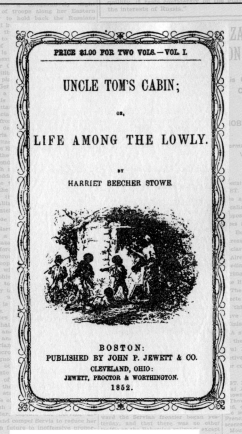

PRICE $1.00 FOR TWO VOLS.—VOL. I.

UNCLE TOM'S CABIN;

OR,

LIFE AMONG THE LOWLY.

BY

HARRIET BEECHER STOWE.

BOSTON:
PUBLISHED BY JOHN P. JEWETT & CO.
CLEVELAND, OHIO:
JEWETT, PROCTOR & WORTHINGTON.
1852.

Uncle Tom's Cabin was an international sensation, selling more than any other book up to that time except the Bible.

The "something" turned out to be *Uncle Tom's Cabin*, an antislavery novel that became an international sensation. There had been scores of published slave narratives, many written by people who'd experienced and escaped slavery, such as Frederick Douglass. Although Stowe was a Northern white woman, her work about the honorable slave named Tom swept over the world and inspired the muckrakers decades later.

In its first year, *Uncle Tom's Cabin* sold three hundred thousand copies in the United States and over one million copies in England. The only book that had ever sold more was the Bible. Stowe's book inspired stage plays, songs, "anti-Tom" (proslavery) novels, and even products like handkerchiefs, lamps, and games. A popular story holds that when Abraham Lincoln met Stowe during the Civil War, he said, "So you're the little woman who wrote the book that started this great war."

Decades after it was published, the book's success lived on as a model of possibility for the muckrakers. When future muckraker Upton Sinclair arrived in Chicago, he supposedly announced that he'd come "to write the *Uncle Tom's Cabin* of the Labor Movement!" Sinclair went on to write *The Jungle*, which told the story of a fictional Lithuanian immigrant named Jurgis Rudkus and his struggle to survive in the new America.

McCLURE'S MAGAZINE.

MAGAZINE.

15 cts.

1.50
a year.

McClure's was *the* muckraking magazine, and it was more affordable than most at 15 cents per issue.

·FOR · SALE · HE[R]

The Storytellers

Much like the vibrant, crowded, and chaotic Lower East Side neighborhood of New York City—where many immigrants lived and where reporters like Jacob Riis focused their energy—the muckraking movement was messy. No list or professional group defined who was or wasn't in the muckraking club. No one date is the absolute start of muckraking. While muckraking articles clearly led to reforms that improved life for millions of people, we can't give credit to one journalist or story for a given reform. There were lots of other people working for reforms back then: activists, social workers, politicians, and others. Their combined efforts were key.

Even if certain parts of the history are a little fuzzy, central muckraking people and organizations emerge from the fog. The heart of the muckraking movement was a magazine called *McClure's*. It was founded by a brilliant, energetic, and charismatic Irish immigrant named Samuel Sidney McClure and his partner, John Sanborn Phillips (who was the steadying influence for the business). The first issue came out in June 1893 and cost fifteen cents per copy—cheaper than most magazines, which cost at least thirty-five cents per copy. The low price shows that McClure and Phillips were striving to reach a mass audience.

McClure had a gift for finding talented writers and convincing them to work for him. At the peak of the muckraking movement, he had the nation's leading investigative journalists on his staff. One of the most important things McClure did to achieve greatness for his magazine was a simple thing: he gave his writers time to work. He let them work on single articles for months and on series of articles for years.

Many people point to the January 1903 edition of *McClure's* as the start of the muckraking period. This issue contained three investigative articles. One was the first article in a series by Ida Tarbell about the history of John D. Rockefeller's monopolistic Standard Oil company. Another was Lincoln Steffen's article "The Shame of Minneapolis," which exposed corruption in that city's government. The third was Raymond Stannard Baker's article "Right to Work," which was about violence between Pennsylvania coal miners on strike and miners who chose not to strike.

Though this issue was the start of a period of intense muckraking in America, "there was already a reform spirit astir in America" when the muckrakers began, says historian James Harvey Young in his 1961 book *The Toadstool Millionaires*. Tarbell, Baker, Steffens, and the others simply "fanned local fires into a searing national flame." One of the best-known earlier journalists who fanned local fires was Jacob Riis.

Jacob Riis

Born in Denmark in 1849, Jacob Riis immigrated to the United States in 1870. At first, he couldn't find work, and he wound up on the streets, begging for food and sleeping overnight in New York City police lodging houses (the homeless shelters of that era, known for being uncomfortable, filthy, and disease-ridden).

One night at a police lodge, someone robbed Riis of a cherished locket. When Riis complained, the policeman on duty didn't believe him, or perhaps didn't care, and tossed Riis out of the station. Worse, the officer beat and killed Riis's canine companion, a little stray. Angered and heartbroken, Riis would forever hate the lodging houses.

Though these events made for a very rough start in America, Riis went on to find work doing odd jobs, as a carpenter, a salesman, and eventually a journalist. In 1877, he landed a job as a crime reporter with the *New York Tribune*.

Riis was a gifted observer and storyteller. He wrote his stories "with heart, humor, and understanding," said Lincoln Steffens. "Beautiful stories they were, sometimes, for Riis could write." On the crime beat, Riis spent virtually all his time in New York's poorest, dirtiest, most crowded neighborhoods. He saw so much misery, and after a while he wanted a harder-hitting way to show what life was like for New York's immigrants. "I wrote," he said in his autobiography, "but it seemed to make no impression." How could he get people to truly see the situation of the poor?

"One morning, scanning my newspaper at the breakfast table, I put it down with an outcry that startled my wife,

This 1895 photo by Jacob Riis shows men in a police station lodging house in New York City. The houses were known for being miserable places, and records say this house carried typhus.

Jacob Riis used modern technology—flash photography—to take this photo of a mother and baby in 1889.

sitting opposite," he said. "There it was, the thing I had been looking for all those years." The four-line article that grabbed his attention described a new way "to take pictures by flashlight."

Riis was thrilled; suddenly he could take photos in the tenements, which had little to no lighting. "The darkest corner might be photographed that way," he wrote. Within a brief time, Riis had his "flashlight." He formed a "raiding party" that, without warning, descended on tenements at night to take pictures:

> The police went along from curiosity; sometimes for protection. For that they were hardly needed. It is not too much to say that our party carried terror wherever it went. The flashlight of those days was contained in cartridges fired from a revolver. The spectacle of half a dozen strange men invading a house in the midnight hour armed with big pistols which they shot off recklessly was hardly reassuring, however sugary our speech, and it was not to be wondered at if the tenants bolted through windows and down fire-escapes wherever we went.

Eventually, Riis started taking photos as a solo act. His images showed homeless children sleeping in stairwells, families working in sweatshops, ragpickers, people sleeping a dozen or twenty to a room, and more.

In 1890, Riis published many of his photos in what is now a landmark Progressive Era book: *How the Other Half Lives*. It was highly praised by readers and reviewers— including New York City's police commissioner, Theodore Roosevelt. Roosevelt and Riis would work together on many city reforms, becoming lifelong friends in the process. (Roosevelt would go from being a police commissioner to governor of New York, vice president of the United States under William McKinley, and, ultimately, America's twenty-sixth president.)

Through writing, photos and slide-show lectures, Riis helped achieve many reforms in New York. These included housing and child-labor laws; new services including garbage, sewers, and water; improvements such as indoor lighting and ventilation; and new playgrounds. Under his urging and with Roosevelt's help, the city shut down police lodges and opened new homeless shelters. "The murder of my dog was avenged," Riis would write.

Riis is sometimes criticized for stereotyping the Irish, Italian, German, Chinese, and other immigrants he wrote about. But he's also given credit for challenging the idea that the poor were lazy and inferior. Today, *How the Other Half Lives* is regarded as a classic of early photojournalism, and Riis's photos are in the Museum of the City of New York, the International Center of Photography, and other museums.

Ida B. Wells

While Riis and other muckrakers focused on problems that grew out of rapid industrialization and urbanization, Ida B. Wells did not. She wrote newspaper articles and pamphlets about racial hatred and one of the most terrible legacies of slavery: lynching, which is a type of murder committed by a mob.

After the Civil War ended, many whites in the South resisted the idea of racial equality and used intimidation and violence to oppress black people. African Americans faced a

IDA B. WELLS.

Muckraker Ida Wells said she didn't need to exaggerate the horrors of lynching: "I do not have to embellish. It makes its own way."

constant threat of being beaten or lynched if they demanded or tried to exercise rights such as the right to vote, or even if they spoke to someone assertively.

As a newspaper editor and investigative journalist in Memphis, Wells confronted this evil through journalism, putting her life at risk. She investigated and exposed hundreds of lynchings, along with the lies Southern white segregationists would tell to justify murder. Angry whites threatened Wells and even at one point stormed her office and trashed it. Fortunately, Wells was away at the time, so she wasn't hurt.

Here's how Wells summed up the injustice as she saw and experienced it:

> The city of Memphis has demonstrated that neither character nor standing avails the Negro if he dares to protect himself against the white man or become his rival. There is nothing we can do about the lynching now, as we are out-numbered and without arms … There is therefore only one thing left that we can do; save our money and leave a town which will neither protect our lives and property, nor give us a fair trial in the courts, but takes us out and murders us in cold blood when accused by white persons.

After Wells wrote the article that included the passage above, many African Americans did heed her advice and move away from Memphis. As more people learned of Wells's crusade against lynching, she received invitations to speak in the North and even in Europe, where her talks helped instigate an antilynching movement.

Wells's articles were published in a newspaper called the *New York Age* and as pamphlets. Among the best known of her pamphlets is *Southern Horrors: Lynch Law in All Its Phases*, which exposed that Southerners often wrongfully accused black men of rape as a method of justifying their lynching.

Although white people sometimes challenged the truthfulness of Wells's accounts of lynching, or questioned if they were exaggerated, Wells stood firm:

> I am only a mouthpiece through which to tell the story of lynching and I have told it so often that I know it by heart. I do not have to embellish; it makes its own way.

Wells resisted romance because she said it would detract from her work. But at age thirty-three, she married Ferdinand L. Barnett, a prominent Chicago lawyer and president of the Illinois antilynching league. The wedding was of great interest to the public, and the *New York Times* even ran a paragraph on its front page. Said the *Times* decades later: "That the nuptials of a black woman, born into slavery thirty-three years earlier, could make the front page of *The Times* [in that era], speaks to a woman who was, by definition, remarkable." Wells was known after her marriage as Ida B. Wells-Barnett. At the time, adopting a hyphenated last name rather than shedding her maiden name altogether was a bold choice.

Barnett had two sons from a previous marriage, and together he and Wells would have four children: Charles, Herman, Ida, and Alfreda. Wells continued to be active professionally even as she raised her children. She kept

Exceptional Muckrakers: Nellie Bly, Stunt Journalist

Born Elizabeth Jane Cochran, journalist and adventurer Nellie Bly was, among all the muckrakers, probably the most larger-than-life. She is best known for her "stunt journalism," stories based on dangerous or difficult challenges. Bly's most famous stunt was to make it around the world (by steamship and train) in seventy-two days, an idea inspired by the character Phileas Fogg in Jules Verne's book *Around the World in Eighty Days*.

The successful stunt made her famous, but she is also known for her fearless muckraking articles, especially the series later published in book form as *Ten Days in a Mad House*. For this sensational piece, Bly posed as a mentally ill patient and was admitted to the Women's Lunatic Asylum on Blackwell's Island in New York. She found and wrote about deplorable conditions and harsh treatment, especially for the poorest women at the asylum. Her exposé led to several improvements at the institution. Bly went on to tackle many other undercover assignments and traveled to Mexico as a foreign correspondent.

When she was thirty-one, she married millionaire manufacturer Robert Seaman. He died of heart problems shortly after being struck by a horse and carriage, and Bly took over his company, Ironclad Manufacturing. Although successful for a time, the company eventually went bankrupt. Bly returned to reporting, covering World War I from the front. She also wrote many stories about the women's suffrage movement.

Muckraker Nellie Bly went undercover to expose terrible conditions at the Women's Lunatic Asylum on Blackwell's Island in New York.

Bly died of pneumonia at the age of fifty-seven. In a tribute column, influential New York editor Arthur Brisbane said that Bly was "the best reporter in America and that is saying a good deal."

writing and worked as an activist for racial justice, women's rights, and, much like Riis, urban reform on behalf of people who had migrated to the city. In this case, she wrote about African Americans who had moved up to Chicago from the South. In 1930, she unsuccessfully ran as an independent candidate for the Illinois state senate. Wells was working on her autobiography, *Crusade for Justice*, when she died of kidney failure in 1931.

Josiah Flynt

As Ida B. Wells was motivated by a thirst for justice, Josiah Flynt was motivated by a thirst for experience and understanding. Was Flynt a journalist who went undercover as a tramp, or was he at heart a tramp who made a living as a journalist? The answer isn't clear, for Flynt was an unusual man. What is clear is that Flynt was a constant traveler (even as a child, he frequently ran away for days, just to wander) as well as a keen and hungry observer of people. He was especially interested in people who lived outside the mainstream of society.

He was born Josiah Flynt Willard in Appleton, Wisconsin, in 1869. His father, a newspaper editor, died when Flynt was a boy. Afterward, despite having a close relationship with his mother, Flynt began misbehaving. Not only did he frequently run off, but he also stole things (even, once, a horse and buggy). Despite being small for his age, he got into fights. When he was a young man, he started "riding the rails," living the life of a hobo, sneaking onto trains and traveling from town to town.

This was during the Long Depression of 1873–1879, when many unemployed men, young and old, rode trains and tramped through the country in search of work or a handout.

Although Flynt tired of the vagrant life after eight months and eventually attended college in Berlin, Germany, he would drop in and out of the tramping world throughout his relatively short life.

But he would also hobnob with the rich and famous. While in Europe, he moved around in high society, and he even met the master writer Leo Tolstoy and playwright Henrik Ibsen.

Flynt was known as a gifted "spy" in whatever new world he infiltrated. For example, he would adjust his gait (the way he walked), gestures, and speaking style to blend in with the hobos he befriended. This talent served him well later, as a journalist who specialized in writing about the underworld and its criminals.

Flynt's most sensational work, *The World of Graft*, exposed crime and corruption in Boston, Chicago, New York, and other cities. The public was fascinated by Flynt's adventures, and the book made Flynt nationally famous.

According to Louis Filler, a leading authority on muckrakers and the author of *Crusaders for American Liberalism*, Flynt's *The World of Graft* was the "first genuine muckraking book." Because it exposed police as well as criminal wrongdoing, the New York police were incensed by it and threatened to retaliate against Flynt. And so, Flynt disappeared for a time, as he was very good at doing.

Flynt was working on a book about poolroom gambling rackets when he got sick and died of pneumonia in 1907. He was probably weakened already, as he had been addicted for years to drugs and alcohol, as well as being a heavy smoker since age nine.

The Associated Press (a news wire service that distributes stories to newspapers) ran this headline when Flynt died: "Josiah Flynt, Tramp, Is Dead in Chicago." Tramp, yes, but he is best remembered as a fearless explorer of human societies high and low.

The Heart of the Movement: Tarbell, Baker, Steffens at *McClure's* Magazine

Though Riis, Wells, and Flynt are important examples of muckrakers, the three reporters most often associated with muckraking (in addition to Upton Sinclair) are Ray Stannard Baker, Ida Tarbell, and Lincoln Steffens.

Ray Stannard Baker

Ray Stannard Baker was one of the earlier muckrakers and a highly esteemed journalist. Not only did he have thousands of fans who enjoyed his articles and books, he also had the ear of President Theodore Roosevelt. Roosevelt courted men like Baker for his own political purposes but also relied on them for information and listened to their opinions, just as, when he was New York's police commissioner, he had relied on Jacob Riis. According to historian Jessica Dorman, Roosevelt once wrote Baker: "You have impressed me with your earnest desire to be fair, with your freedom from hysteria, and with your anxiety to tell the truth rather than to write something that will be sensational."

Baker wrote hundreds of articles covering virtually all areas of reformers' focus, including labor union activity, urban poverty, racial oppression, and corruption in city government. His book *Following the Color Line* examined race relations in Atlanta after race riots there, and he wrote one of three muckraking articles featured in the famous January 1903 issue of *McClure's*.

Like the best muckrakers, Baker could win the confidence of people from all walks of life. "During his best years as a journalist he was known as the greatest reporter in America," said Filler. In his later career, Baker went to work for President Woodrow Wilson, eventually acting as Wilson's press secretary during peace talks in Europe after World War I. He would go on to write an eight-volume biography of Wilson, two volumes of which won the Pulitzer Prize, journalism's top honor.

Like several of the leading muckrakers, Baker was a gifted writer. He published essays and fiction—much of it about rural life—under the name of David Grayson. Many people regard his book *Adventures in Contentment* as a classic work that offers a quiet and gentle wisdom.

Baker died of a heart attack in Amherst, Massachusetts, in 1946.

Ida Tarbell

Ida Tarbell is perhaps the most accomplished and widely respected muckraker. She was a highly intelligent, industrious individual, happiest when intellectually challenged and doing meaningful work. During her twenties, she was a writer and editor for a small paper in Pennsylvania when she decided to move to Paris and make a living writing articles for American magazines about French people and culture.

In Paris, she barely got by at first, but eventually she lined up enough assignments to pay the rent. One day, a man knocked on the door of her apartment. It was Samuel McClure. He had read her articles and was quite impressed. Would she like to write for *McClure's*?

McClure often captivated people with his vision, passion, and personality. He and Tarbell talked for three hours that night. Eventually, Tarbell started writing articles for *McClure's*, including a popular article on Napoleon Bonaparte.

Ida Tarbell was a respected investigative journalist whose exposé led to the breakup of the monopolistic Standard Oil Company.

She followed this success with a return to the United States and a series of biographical articles on Abraham Lincoln that cleverly included lesser-known information about the early life of America's most beloved president. *McClure's* readers ate them up. The articles not only made Tarbell nationally famous, they doubled the number of people who subscribed to *McClure's*. Tarbell eventually expanded her work on Lincoln into eight books.

The work that Tarbell is most famous for is a nineteen-part investigative work about John D. Rockefeller's Standard Oil Company. This exhaustively researched investigation helped lead to the breakup of Rockefeller's monopoly on the oil industry.

Interestingly, Tarbell's own father had been an independent oil producer whose business suffered because of Rockefeller's anticompetitive business practices. These practices were specifically designed to drive smaller producers into bankruptcy and included secret deals between the railroad companies and Rockefeller.

The History of the Standard Oil Company would establish Tarbell's place in the annals of US business and social history. Although she took pains to be fair and make sure every fact she included was accurate, she did not shy away from expressing her opinion that "our national life is on every side distinctly poorer, uglier, meaner, for the kind of influence [Rockefeller] exercises."

Today Tarbell's Standard Oil series is regarded as one of the most important pieces of journalism ever written.

Lincoln Steffens

Lincoln Steffens was working as an editor at *McClure's* when Samuel McClure told him to get out of the office and out of New York. To be a worthwhile editor with promising ideas, Steffens would have to see the world. "Get out of here, travel, go—somewhere," Steffens would remember McClure saying to him. "Buy a railroad ticket, get on a train, and there, where it lands you, there you will learn to edit a magazine."

Exceptional Muckrakers: Edwin Markham, Poet

The muckrakers were not all journalists; some wrote novels and poetry. Edwin Markham's poem "The Man with a Hoe," published in 1899 and translated into thirty-seven languages, is about the bleak, hard life of a working man. It was inspired by a French painting depicting a laborer in a field, stooped over a hoe and looking dulled and weary.

Markham first read the poem at a New Year's Eve party, which led to its being published in the *San Francisco Examiner*. The poem caused a sensation in the United States, generating much discussion about issues of wealth, privilege, poverty, the sins of the age, and socialism.

Said Louis Filler in *Crusaders for American Liberalism*, "'The Man with the Hoe' was praised and quoted and reprinted. It was hailed by educators and critics as the greatest poem of the century and one of the greatest poems ever written." The poem was so widely shared and discussed that railroad magnate Collis P. Huntington asked: "Is America going to turn to Socialism over one poem?"

America did not, and somewhat ironically for a poem with socialist undertones, the poem was an income source for Markham, who began touring and lecturing after it was published. When Markham died, the *New York Times* noted the poet had earned more than $200,000 from "The Man

Edwin Markham's muckraking poem "The Man with a Hoe" was inspired by this French painting depicting a weary laborer in a field.

with the Hoe" over his lifetime, making it probably the most profitable poem ever. Markham also wrote nonfiction, including coauthoring a 1914 book about child labor and the need for reform.

Steffens would stay out in the cities of America, especially in its heartland, for more than two years. He wanted to catch the pulse of the country. Writes historian Doris Kearns Goodwin:

> Following up on *McClure's* persistent interest in political corruption, Steffens interviewed city editors, political bosses, crusading district attorneys, and reformist mayors. In each city, he uncovered an invisible web of power linking political bosses to both the criminal world below and the business community above.

Steffens's series of articles on corruption in city and state politics, which were first run in *McClure's* and then compiled in a book called *The Shame of the Cities*, would help end the era of political bosses. Like Tarbell's *The History of the Standard Oil Company*, this work is regarded as one of the finest works in American journalism history.

Steffens's arsenal of talents included talking to people and asking questions in a way that got results. William Randolph Hearst, owner of the *New York Journal* and a man not easily intimidated or impressed, said Steffens was one of the most effective interviewers he had ever encountered.

Steffens was a leader among journalists and had many protégés, including John Reed, who would become famous after witnessing and writing about the Bolshevik revolution in Russia. Steffens also counted among his friends one of the greatest writers in modern Western history: James Joyce. Lincoln Steffens died at the age of seventy, in 1936.

"I aimed at the public's heart, and by accident I hit it in the stomach," said Upton Sinclair about his muckraking book *The Jungle*.

Upton Sinclair

Upton Beall Sinclair was born September 20, 1878, in Baltimore, Maryland. His early life was not easy: his father was an alcoholic, while his mother was strict and unyielding. Though his family was poor, his grandparents were wealthy. As a boy, he noticed the difference in household comfort and lifestyles.

Perhaps at least partly because of this early experience, Sinclair had strong socialist views as an adult. His novel *The Jungle*—which is the most famous example of muckraking journalism—first appeared as a series in the socialist newspaper *Appeal to Reason*.

The Jungle tells the dismal, harrowing story of a Lithuanian immigrant named Jurgis Rudkus who works in a Chicago slaughterhouse. It describes tenement living, backbreaking working conditions, and predatory men who exploit new immigrants. Rudkus and his family only want a fair shot, simply a chance to work hard and make a better life. But the forces of greed and cruelty hammer down their honorable intentions.

The Jungle is most famous for describing disgusting, unsanitary conditions in the meatpacking facilities. Book publisher Doubleday printed *The Jungle* after it appeared in *Appeal to Reason*, and Sinclair became famous virtually overnight. The book came out in February, and by April, Theodore Roosevelt was hosting Sinclair at the White House. Although Roosevelt did not approve of the book's socialist message, he did respond to the food-safety problems *The Jungle* exposed by dispatching investigators to the Chicago stockyards and meat factories.

In the end, Sinclair's book directly led to the Pure Food and Drug Act of 1906, which set rules designed to make meat (and medicine) safer, as well as the Meat Inspection Act, which among other things requires inspection of all livestock for disease before slaughter. Beyond his writing, Sinclair also attempted to shape politics from within the government. He organized a reform movement during the Great Depression and ran for office multiple times, including running for Congress in 1906. Though he never won a campaign, his attempts shaped policies of the era, namely Franklin D. Roosevelt's New Deal.

Sinclair was a prolific writer, meaning he wrote many books quickly. By the time he died in 1968, he had written about ninety books. These included a series of eleven novels about a character named Lanny Budd who travels the world and often is on the scene of momentous events. One of these books, *Dragon's Teeth*, set during the Nazi period in Germany, won the Pulitzer Prize in 1943.

Sinclair died at the age of ninety in a New Jersey nursing home. He is buried in Rock Creek cemetery in Washington, DC.

The twenty-sixth president of the United States, Theodore Roosevelt, coined the term "muckraker" and guided the nation through years of important reforms.

Stories That Shaped America

3

Determined to make a difference by shining a light on hidden or ignored problems, the muckrakers wrote thousands of articles about areas of society that needed reform. Once they'd published their stories, they believed, it was up to the people to insist on change and then for government to act. In other words, they believed in the power of the press to nudge a democratic society into being fairer and, in the end, kinder. A saying attributed to a popular political figure of the day, Governor Al Smith of New York, goes something like this: "The cure for the evils of democracy is more democracy." The muckrakers were a big part of that "more."

Writing Wrongs: How They Got the Story

Investigative journalists today—the modern muckrakers—let facts speak for themselves. They don't scold or preach; they simply report. The muckraking journalists of the Progressive

Era were a bit different. Muckrakers' writing sometimes expressed anger at injustice, sorrow about people's suffering, and impatience at the slow pace or lack of reform. Sometimes, too, they used the sensationalizing methods associated with yellow journalism: dramatic story angles and big, bold headlines.

But, like today's investigative journalists, the leading muckrakers of the Progressive Era made sure their stories were accurate. Because they were "naming names," meaning they exposed the wrongdoing of specific individuals or groups, they had to have their facts straight. Then and now, reporters had to take care to avoid destroying a person's good name and being sued for libel, which is the act of publishing lies and tarnishing someone's reputation.

Tarbell, Steffens, Baker, and other reform journalists confirmed the facts they reported and backed up their conclusions with "hard data," such as statistics. Here's an example from Riis's book *How the Other Half Lives*. He was writing about how the crowded and dirty tenements led to disease.

> In one cholera epidemic that scarcely touched the clean wards [or areas of the city], the tenants died at the rate of one hundred and ninety-five to the thousand of population; which forced the general mortality of the city up from 1 in 41.83 in 1815, to 1 in 27.33 in 1855.

He then puts the crowding in a global perspective:

> The tenement house population had swelled to half a million souls … and on the East Side, in what is

still the most densely populated district in all the world, China not excluded, it was packed at the rate of 290,000 to the square mile.

Tools of the Trade

Statistics (like those Riis cited) and other hard facts give an article credibility. Getting those facts could be an onerous process. Much of muckrakers' reporting relied on paper trails. Court records are one example. Oftentimes the muckrakers simply gathered and wrote about information that was freely available. Says David Mark Chalmers, author of *The Social and Political Ideas of Muckrakers*, "They did not uncover corruption—although there were notable original exposures—as much as they brought before the public eye the mountainous details of graft which crowded the public records."

But the muckrakers also used other, more dramatic tools of trade, such as going undercover or being on the scene of a labor strike. They also had to be skilled interviewers who could get the people they interviewed (known as "sources") to trust them, and they had to know where to find expert opinions and when to use them.

Finally, and perhaps this was the key to their success, they had to have "heart"—outrage at the sight of children working in coal mines, horror at the working conditions faced by meatpackers, compassion for families living twelve to a room, anger at big business putting the little operators out of business without a care. They had to have a fervent desire to right wrongs so they could use their immense energy and talents to "write wrongs."

The Appeal
of Patent Medicines

Patent medicines—whose use in the United States began back in the colonial era—were products sold and advertised as medicine. They didn't require a doctor's prescription, and often a single product claimed to cure many ailments, even incurable conditions like cancer or heart disease. They had names that were distinctive, such as Dr. Rowell's Celebrated Invigorating Tonic; sounded magical, such as Hamlin's Wizard Oil; or hinted at the exotic (at least to many American ears), such as Qina Laroche: The Great French Tonic or Peruvian Syrup.

Although they succeeded in lining the pockets of their makers, they were generally less effective as medicines. Quite often, they were useless or even harmful. In the second half of the 1800s, the number of patent medicines exploded, along with their advertisements promising health and vigor, hair growth, fat reduction, a good night's sleep, happiness, and more.

Although newspaper editors most likely knew these medicines to be bogus, they relied on income from patent advertisements. Few editors, rural or urban, refused to run them. (The exceptions included muckraker William Allen White, who banned all such ads from his Kansas paper, the *Emporia Gazette*.)

Besides running ads in newspapers and magazines, patent medicine manufacturers put up billboard ads, sent out free samples, and published their own homey-looking almanacs.

Why were so many people drawn to patent medicines? Part of their appeal, say historians, related to people's wariness

This ad for Ayer's Sarsaparilla is one of many patent medicine ads that claimed to cure a lengthy list of conditions.

about medicine at the time. Doctors often used bloodletting, forced vomiting, sweating, and other harsh treatments meant to shock the body into a stronger state. Not surprisingly, people wanted to avoid that pain and risk.

Going Undercover

Going undercover means withholding your name and role as a reporter and possibly (probably) pretending to be someone else. Muckrakers who went undercover to get the story include two of the best known: Upton Sinclair and Nellie Bly.

Upton Sinclair in Chicago

Asked by an editor to investigate the plight of workers in the meatpacking industry, Sinclair traveled to Chicago in 1904 and spent seven weeks in and around the meatpacking plants. (Meatpacking refers to the slaughter of cows and other animals and the preparing and packaging of the meat for sale.) For those weeks, Sinclair would later write, he "went about, white faced and thin, partly from undernourishment, partly from horror."

Sinclair wandered the yards during the day, observing and taking mental notes. "My friends would risk their jobs to show me what I wanted to see," he wrote. He tried to blend in, so no one would question why he was lurking about:

> I was not much better dressed then the workers, and found that by the simple device of carrying a dinner pail I could go anywhere. So long as I kept moving, no one would heed me. When I wanted to make careful observations, I would pass again and again through the same room.

At night, he would visit the workers in their homes. "They told me their stories, one after one, and I made notes of everything," he said. He also sought out information beyond the walls of the stockyards, talking to experts such as Chicago lawyers, doctors, police, politicians, and others.

Upton Sinclair exposed horrific conditions at meatpacking factories like this sausage factory in Chicago, shown in a photo taken in about 1893.

As he learned new facts and reached new conclusions, he checked his findings with the meatpackers.

The outcome of all this research, Sinclair's *The Jungle*, described terrible hardships: twelve-hour working days, low wages, and factory accidents that mangled limbs. Bosses were indifferent to workers' injuries, sicknesses, or even deaths, and the company did not pay compensation for any of the conditions that workers suffered as a result of their jobs.

When it came to capturing readers' attention and stirring up their emotions, however, terrible labor conditions didn't stand a chance against guts, blood, and filth. After reading *The Jungle*, everyone wanted to discuss one thing: unclean meat. Readers were horrified by Sinclair's descriptions of diseased cows being slaughtered for meat, guts being swept off filthy floors to be packed into cans as tinned meat, rats being ground up with offal (the parts of an animal that usually aren't eaten, such as gristle) into sausage. Here's a sample:

> The meat would be shoveled into carts, and the man who did the shoveling would not trouble to lift out a rat even when he saw one … There was no place for the men to wash their hands before they ate their dinner, and so they made a practice of washing them in the water that was to be ladled into the sausage. There were the butt-ends of smoked meat, and the scraps of corned beef, and all the odds and ends of the waste of the plants, that would be dumped into old barrels in the cellar and left there … In the barrels would be dirt and rust and old nails and stale water—and cartload after cartload of it would be taken up and dumped into

THE JUNGLE

BY
UPTON SINCLAIR

DOUBLEDAY, PAGE & C?
NEW YORK

The Jungle tells of a Lithuanian man who simply wants a chance to work hard and realize the American dream but is crushed by forces, including society's indifference to the plight of immigrants.

the hoppers with fresh meat, and sent out to the public's breakfast.

Very famously, Sinclair would lament about the reaction to his book, "I aimed at the public's heart, and by accident I hit it in the stomach."

Perhaps it's not surprising that *The Jungle* prompted quick action on the part of Theodore Roosevelt. *The Jungle* would not only lead to new laws requiring food safety, it would stand for more than a century—through today—as the leading example of muckraking journalism.

Nellie Bly at Blackwell's

Bly was not the only journalist to go undercover into a Victorian asylum (a hospital for mentally ill people), but she is the best known. In the nineteenth and early twentieth centuries, asylums were notorious for horrendous conditions. As a twenty-three-year-old reporter, Bly was given the assignment by her editor and immediately went home to practice giving the appearance of someone mentally ill. She rehearsed strange faces in the mirror and stayed up all night reading ghost stories to put herself in an anxious state.

She managed to convince authorities she was insane by appearing dazed, talking nonsensically, and claiming she did not remember where she came from. Once admitted into the Women's Lunatic Asylum on Blackwell's Island, she saw women patients being practically starved, kept in freezing conditions, and physically abused by hospital staff members:

The water was ice-cold, and I again began to protest. How useless it all was! ... Suddenly I got, one after the other, three buckets of water over my head–ice-cold water, too–into my eyes, my ears, my nose and my mouth. I think I experienced some of the sensations of a drowning person as they dragged me, gasping, shivering and quaking, from the tub. For once I did look insane. I caught a glance of the indescribable look on the faces of my companions, who had witnessed my fate and knew theirs was surely following. Unable to control myself at the absurd picture I presented, I burst into roars of laughter. They put me, dripping wet, into a short canton flannel slip, labeled across the extreme end in large black letters, "Lunatic Asylum, B. I., H. 6." The letters meant Blackwell's Island, Hall 6.

She also met women who were imprisoned on the island for being mentally ill, when their real "problem" was that they were immigrants who didn't speak English well or at all—officials couldn't understand what they were saying.

Bly's shocking story led to a grand jury investigation and significant improvements at Blackwell's. It also convinced the city to increase its funding for asylums by almost $1 million. And it launched the muckraking and stunt journalism career of a truly remarkable person, Nellie Bly.

Being on the Scene

Perhaps nothing brings a news article to life as much as the details reporters take in by being on the scene. By covering events in person, reporters can record what they see, hear, feel, and even smell and taste. They can observe details such as people's tones of voice and facial expressions,

Unemployed men—members of Coxey's Army—
listen to a speaker during their march to Washington,
DC, to demand jobs.

and when facts are in dispute about what happened—for example, at a labor protest that turned violent—they are detached witnesses.

Being on the scene was especially important for the muckrakers trying to paint a picture of the poor neighborhoods in big cities or the cruel conditions inside factories. Jacob Riis's articles would not have been as effective if he had not been on the scene to report and write passages such as this one:

> I came upon a couple of youngsters in a Mulberry Street yard a while ago that were chalking on the fence their first lesson in "writin'." And this is what they wrote: "Keeb of te Grass." They had it by heart, for there was not, I verily believe, a green sod within a quarter of a mile.

Being an observant eyewitness also helped Riis get results, according to Doris Kearns Goodwin. "When he narrated a suicide, fire, or outbreak of disease," she writes in her book *The Bully Pulpit*, "Jacob Riis took down every detail of the building or the city block where it occurred, relentlessly pursuing the negligent landlords, holding them responsible for the abhorrent conditions and threatening further stories until the problems were redressed."

Being on the scene was a big part of muckraker Ray Stannard Baker's reporting.

In 1894, he covered "Coxey's Army," a protest in which unemployed men marched to Washington, DC, to demand jobs. Jacob S. Coxey wanted his "army" of marchers to serve as a "human petition" for a government program that would put men to work building roads. Like much of America, Baker was unsympathetic to their cause—initially. After several days marching alongside the men, according to Goodwin, Baker's tone changed: "These were not 'bums, tramps, and vagabonds' but 'genuine farmers and workingmen,' driven in a time of depression by their inability to 'earn a living.'"

One of Baker's most well-known articles discusses the way in which striking Pennsylvania coal miners abused men who chose to work instead of strike. A strike can only really be effective for a labor union if the company is forced to shut down or cut back on operations. If people still show up to work, they sabotage the strike. Strikers call workers who cross the strikers' picket line "scabs."

Baker visited miners in their homes in eastern Pennsylvania to gain their trust and find out what had happened. He uncovered disturbing stories about non-striking miners being beaten, even killed, and families driven from their homes, which were sometimes burned to the ground.

Baker visited a mother of miners whose non-striking son was badly beaten. She "spoke with pride" of her sons, but when the subject of her non-striking son, John, came up, "she flushed at the mention of his name, said at first that she would have nothing to say about him, and then, bitterly: 'He might better be dead, for he's brought disgrace on the name … He deserved all he got … He wasn't raised a scab.'"

These are the kinds of startling statements that, as a rule, come only from in-person conversations and require a good deal of interviewing skill.

There is a better-known example of the way being on the scene can help journalists write powerfully. It was during the Triangle Shirtwaist Factory fire. When the Shirtwaist workers had no choice but to jump out of the ninth-story window because the flames were at their backs, a United Press reporter on the scene wrote: "Thud—dead; thud—dead; thud—dead; thud—dead. Sixty-two thud—deads. I call them that, because the sound and the thought of death came to me each time, at the same instant." In a moment such as this, a journalist's words can be a needed outlet for the public's grief, outrage, and horror.

"Theodore Roosevelt: A Character Sketch," by Ray Stannard Baker

Capturing ordinary visual and other details is another way being on the scene helps journalists write powerfully. Not only were muckrakers able to add credibility to their stories by reporting about what they saw and heard, but they could also create greater interest and help readers feel that they were on the scene themselves. Here is an example of this kind of scenic reporting, from Ray Stannard Baker:

> In 1886, Mr. [Theodore] Roosevelt married Miss Edith Kermit Carow, and they have five children, three sons and two daughters. Their home is at Sagamore Hill, about three miles [4.8 kilometers] from Oyster Bay, on Long Island Sound. A big, roomy, comfortable house stands on the top of the hill. Wide, green vistas open in front, so that a visitor sitting in one of the hospitable chairs on the veranda may see miles of wooded, watered country, a view unsurpassed anywhere on Long Island Sound. The rooms within everywhere give

Another Reality

Muckraker Jacob Riis was a gifted writer, but it was his photographs that catapulted to new heights his stories about poor immigrants living in New York City's Lower East Side. He often visited tenements at night as a reporter for the *New York Tribune* (and later the *New York Evening Sun*). "The sights I saw there gripped my heart until I felt that I must tell of them, or burst," Riis wrote in his autobiography.

He saw children who were dying from the foul air in apartments that had no air shafts. He found families being exploited by landlords who drastically overcharged them for unbelievably overcrowded slums. In one case, five families were sharing a room that was 12 feet (3.7 meters) by 19 feet (5.8 m). In another, an African American family was living in a room that was "three short steps across either way [at] its full extent." Often, Riis encountered rents that were 25 to 30 percent higher than in uptown buildings.

Though Riis wrote about the tenements, "it seemed to make no impression," he said. The answer to his dilemma proved to be new technology: the flash. At that time, it took photographers many minutes, even a half hour, to capture images on acetate film. Subjects had to keep still, or the figures in the picture would blur. Also, because the tenements were so dark, Riis found it impossible to take decent photos. But with the flash, Riis could capture the scene.

The magnesium-based flash powder Riis used was called Blitzlichtpulver. This commercial product appeared after magnesium became more affordable than it had been

Flash technology helped bring about progressive reforms because suddenly photographers could show society the awful state of dark, dirty, overcrowded tenements. This photo shows an early flash camera.

previously. The formula consisted of magnesium and a chlorate (the oxidizer) that made a mini-explosion when ignited, emitting a bright light that allowed photographers to capture photos at a quick shutter speed—in other words, in darker conditions. The kind of flash technology Riis used came in cartridges fired from a sort of pistol.

The flash powder had drawbacks. It was an explosive, and photographers on the job sometimes were burned or even had fatal accidents before safer technology—flash bulbs—came along in the 1920s. In addition, the flash powder released a cloud after being fired, which could fall all around the room and dust people and objects. This byproduct was a nuisance, prevented clear photos after the first had been taken, and was unhealthy to breathe in.

The photos that appeared in Riis's articles and, later, in his landmark book *How the Other Half Lives* shocked America. Said Tom Brokaw in a History Channel interview: "Those photographs came out at a time when America was saying to the world, 'This is the golden destination.' And what he demonstrated was that there was another reality. There were some deplorable living conditions, and this country was not just forced to confront those conditions, but then was moved to begin to deal with them."

evidence, in the skins of bears and bison and the splendid antlers of elk and deer, of Mr. Roosevelt's prowess as a hunter. The library is rich with the books of which he is most fond—history, standard literature, and hunting. Portraits of the three greatest Americans, Lincoln, Washington, and Grant, have the place of honor over the cases, and there are numerous spirited animal compositions in bronze by [Edward Kemeys], the American sculptor. Here Mr. Roosevelt lives and works.

More Than Talk

Another important muckraker tool was interviewing. Lincoln Steffens was such a gifted interviewer that supposedly he could get people to share their own crimes. Says *Bully Pulpit* author Goodwin: "Observers would … credit Steffens's success as a journalist to his 'supreme gift for making men tell—or try to tell—him the truth.' He always seemed to be able to coax people to 'explain themselves,' even when their explanations implicated rather than vindicated them."

For *The History of the Standard Oil Company*, Ida Tarbell interviewed Henry H. Rogers, the leading boss under Rockefeller at the behemoth company. They were introduced to each other by a mutual acquaintance, none other than Mark Twain, and would meet regularly over two years. During these meetings, Tarbell asked Rogers to verify or explain more about what she was uncovering. Rogers seemed happy to explain how Standard Oil operated and made decisions. Some people think that Rogers may have expected Tarbell to write a positive article about Standard Oil. He defended the company as a model of efficiency, and in fact Tarbell did recognize that Standard Oil was built on smart business practices, even as she exposed its lack of fairness. She titled her seventeenth chapter "The Legitimate Greatness of the Standard Oil Company."

As previously mentioned, Tarbell's series of articles appeared in *McClure's* in nineteen installments. Though Tarbell exposed Standard Oil's unethical business practices, Rogers continued to meet with her even after the first stories ran. During these later meetings, according to journalist Gilbert King in *Smithsonian* magazine:

> His face went white with rage to find that Tarbell had uncovered documents that showed the company was still colluding with the railroads to snuff out its competition. "Where did you get that stuff?" Rogers said angrily, pointing to the magazine. Tarbell informed him that his claims of "legitimate competition" were false. "You know this bookkeeping record is true," she told him.

As for Rockefeller, he was displeased about the exposé, argued privately that the article was unfair, and called Tarbell "that misguided woman." But no one ever seriously challenged the story. This was largely due to her painstaking research, including her interviews with Rogers.

Tarbell conducted so much research that she wrote with confidence about Rockefeller's inner motivations:

> To know every detail of the oil trade, to be able to reach at any moment its remotest point, to control even its weakest factor—this was John D. Rockefeller's ideal of doing business. It seemed to be an intellectual necessity for him to be able to direct the course of any particular gallon of oil

from the moment it gushed from the earth until it went into the lamp of a housewife. There must be nothing—nothing in his great machine he did not know to be working right. It was to complete this ideal, to satisfy this necessity, that he undertook, late in the seventies, to organize the oil markets of the world, as he had already organized oil refining and oil transporting. Mr. Rockefeller was driven to this new task of organization not only by his own curious intellect; he was driven to it by that thing so abhorrent to his mind—competition. If, as he claimed, the oil business belonged to him, and if, as he had announced, he was prepared to refine all the oil that men would consume, it followed as a corollary that the markets of the world belonged to him.

In the end, the US government sued Standard Oil for breaking laws against anticompetitive practices. The case went all the way to the US Supreme Court, which found that Standard Oil was in violation of the Sherman Antitrust Act (a law designed to prevent monopolies). Standard Oil was forced to break up into smaller companies.

Great American Fraud

Dr. Lapponi

Physician to the Late Pope Leo XIII., and Now Physician in Ordinary to Pope Pius X., Finds

BUFFALO LITHIA WATER

Of "Marvelous Efficacy in Gout, Rhuematism, Gastro-intestinal Dyspepsia, Gravel, and in all the Various Forms of Uric Acid Diathesis."

If You Are Afflicted With DEAFNESS

Get Our Specially Prepared

PURE Rattlesnake Oil

Dr. Williams' Pink Pills for Pale People

Before the Progressive Era, companies that made so-called health tonics and cures didn't get into trouble for exaggerating or lying about the healing properties of their products—therefore, exaggerate and lie they did.

This was the time of patent medicines, also called nostrums, which were over-the-counter medicines. Muckraking magazines including *Ladies' Home Journal* and *Collier's* published many articles about the ways patent medicines were dangerous or ineffective. Eventually, *Ladies' Home Journal* editor Edward Bok hired a lawyer-turned-journalist named Mark Sullivan to uncover the truth about these so-called drugs. (Editorial decisions led to the exposé's publication in *Collier's* instead of Bok's magazine.) Posing undercover as someone interested in making money from nostrums, Sullivan interviewed chemists, salesmen, and others involved in the patent medicine trade. Among other findings, he discovered that patent medicine manufacturers used "muzzle clauses" in their advertising contracts with newspapers. These clauses said that if a state passed a law banning nostrums, the advertising contract was dead. It was a clever way to get newspaper editors to remain silent about the need for such legislation.

The editor of *Collier's* then hired a freelance writer named Samuel Hopkins Adams. Adams was a muckraker who frequently wrote for *McClure's*. To investigate patent medicines, Adams did an intense amount of research over several months. He gathered and studied patent medicine advertisements, had patent medicines tested by chemists to determine their real ingredients, and consulted medical experts about the healing properties of those ingredients.

The patent medicine makers did not want Adams to proceed with his article and even tried, without success, to blackmail him.

The first of Adams's eleven articles about patent medicines ran in *Collier's* on October 7, 1905. In his first lines, Adams pulled no punches:

> Gullible America will spend this year some seventy-five millions of dollars in the purchase of patent medicines. In consideration of this sum it will swallow huge quantities of alcohol, an appalling amount of opiates and narcotics, a wide assortment of varied drugs ranging from powerful and dangerous heart depressants to insidious liver stimulants; and, far in excess of all other ingredients, undiluted fraud. For fraud, exploited by the skillfulest of advertising bunco men, is the basis of the trade.

Adams found patent medicines that had no healing properties at all. One drug he had analyzed, for example, was simply sugar. An antiseptic named Liquozone was mostly water. Many of the most dangerous medicines were addictive. A popular one named Peruna, for example, tested at about 28 percent alcohol. Adams quotes a doctor:

> I have in the last two years met four cases of persons who drank Peruna in large quantities to intoxication. This was given to them originally as a tonic. They were treated under my care as simple alcoholics.

Other medicines, especially those sold as cough and consumptive (tuberculosis) cures or "soothing syrups," contained opium and cocaine. These "subtle poisons," Adams wrote, "are the most dangerous of all quack medicines, not only in their immediate effect, but because they create enslaving appetites." One father spoke to Adams of his daughter, who had been given an opium-based medicine as a girl, to treat her diarrhea. She became addicted, and at nineteen years old she "was a complete wreck in every way as a result of the opium habit. The father told me, with tears in his eyes, that he would rather she had died with the original illness than to have lived to become the creature which she then was."

Adams's articles, reprinted in book form as *The Great American Fraud*, brought pressure on Congress to pass a law controlling patent medicines. But the top lawmaker in the House, Joe Cannon, refused to bring the bill to the floor for a vote. Finally, however, he had to act because of pressure to regulate the meat industry. The law that finally passed was the Pure Food and Drug Act of 1906.

Muckraking Cartoonist: Thomas Nast

As we have seen already, muckrakers came in many forms, cartoonists included. One of the earlier political cartoonists who focused on corruption in government was Thomas Nast. He used his drawings in *Harper's Weekly* to draw public attention to the crimes of a hugely influential politician known as Boss Tweed (Tweed's first name was actually William). Tweed held state offices, but he was most known as boss of Tammany Hall, the Democratic Party political machine in New York City.

Alive between 1840 and 1902, Nast was active earlier than the muckrakers of the Progressive Era, but his cartoons and their targets illustrate the kind of rampant corruption that bled over into the Progressive Era. In a series of cartoons, Nast skewered Tweed for skimming money here, there, and everywhere. Today, it's estimated Tweed stole millions of dollars—some people say as much as $200 million.

Tweed was indifferent to articles about him. "I don't care a straw for newspaper articles," he said. "My constituents don't know how to read. But they can't help seeing them damn pictures."

Tweed sent emissaries to bribe Nast to give up his cartoon campaign, but Nast laughed them away.

One of Nast's most famous cartoons, "Who Stole the People's Money?" is credited with helping bring about the fall of Boss Tweed, who was eventually arrested, tried, and jailed. Later, after one escape, Tweed was rearrested, and he ultimately died in jail.

According to the *New York Times*, "Who Stole the People's Money?" is "among the most reproduced, mimicked, and well known of all American political cartoons."

A portrait of Boss Tweed, corrupt boss of Tammany Hall

According to the *New York Times*, this cartoon by Thomas Nast is among the most reproduced and well-known political cartoons in American history. It highlights Boss Tweed's wrongdoings.

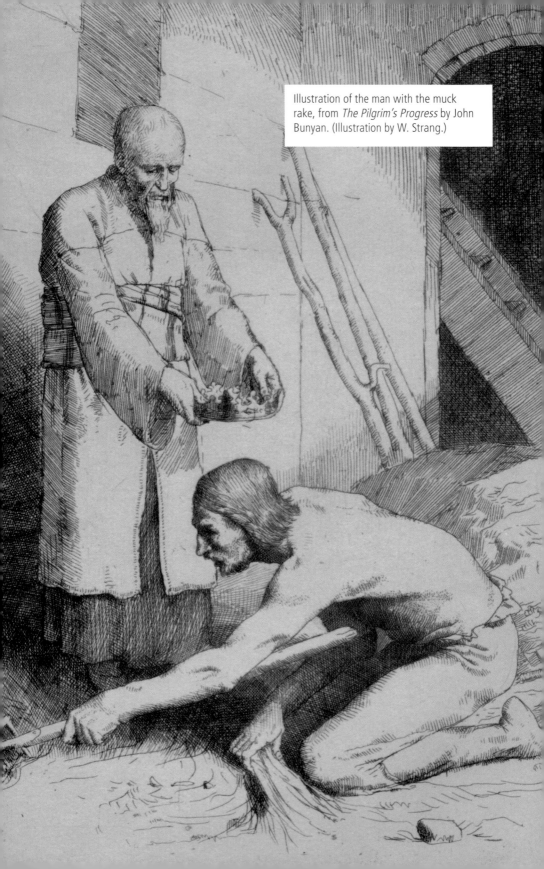
Illustration of the man with the muck rake, from *The Pilgrim's Progress* by John Bunyan. (Illustration by W. Strang.)

The Muckrakers Leave Their Mark

The reform journalists of the Progressive Era didn't name themselves "muckrakers." President Theodore Roosevelt named them that in a speech on April 14, 1906, during a ceremony for a new congressional building.

Treason of the Senate

The muckraking magazine *Cosmopolitan* had recently started a series that exposed corruption in the United States Senate. *Cosmopolitan* was owned by William Randolph Hearst, who at the time was serving in the House of Representatives. The series, "The Treason of the Senate" by journalist and novelist David Graham Phillips, discussed the hidden influence that big business had on US senators. That influence included bribing the lawmakers to vote a certain way, such as for lower taxes on businesses. Senators were apt to be bought by powerful business interests because at that time they were appointed by the states, rather than elected by the people.

Having states appoint US senators created a problem in addition to corruption. Conflict between political groups such as the Democratic and Republican Parties often prevented them from agreeing on who should be named senator. The result was often a deadlock, meaning no senator was appointed.

According to the US Senate:

> Intimidation and bribery marked some of the states' selection of senators. Nine bribery cases were brought before the Senate between 1866 and 1906. In addition, forty-five deadlocks occurred in twenty states between 1891 and 1905, resulting in numerous delays in seating senators. In 1899, problems in electing a senator in Delaware were so acute that the state legislature did not send a senator to Washington for four years.

By exposing problems and corruption in America's top lawmaking body, "The Treason of the Senate" would be one of the farthest-reaching works of muckraking journalism. It helped lead to the passage of the Seventeenth Amendment, which says that senators must be directly elected by the people instead of chosen by state legislators. This change made senators less apt to be bought by powerful business interests, and it solved the problem with deadlocks as well.

With his exposé, Phillips put the muckrakers' spotlight on men Roosevelt knew and respected, including some of his friends. Many believe Roosevelt was reacting to "The Treason of the Senate" when he made his speech "The Man with the Muck-Rake." Roosevelt supposedly told Ray Stannard Baker as much.

The Man with the Muck-rake

In his speech, Roosevelt talked about a book by the seventeenth-century Puritan John Bunyan, *Pilgrim's Progress*. The story includes a passage about a man who is so focused on worldly rather than spiritual matters—cleaning his floor—that he ignores a beautiful celestial crown in his other hand:

> You may recall the description of the Man with the Muck-rake, the man who could look no way but downward, with the muck-rake in his hand; who was offered a celestial crown for his muck-rake, but who would neither look up nor regard the crown he was offered, but continued to rake to himself the filth of the floor.

While conceding the importance of identifying problems in society, Roosevelt went on to liken Bunyan's character with journalists who shine their light only in the darkest and dirtiest corners, saying:

> The man who never does anything else, who never thinks or speaks or writes, save of his feats with the muck-rake, speedily becomes, not a help to society, not an incitement to good, but one of the most potent forces for evil.

Constant stories about corruption and a single-minded focus on wrongdoing do not benefit the nation, Roosevelt argued. If a story is false, then readers may regard the next article as false, even if it exposes important truths. "The soul of every scoundrel is gladdened whenever an honest man is assailed, or even when a scoundrel is untruthfully

Modern-Day Muckrakers

Woodward and Bernstein are the most famous modern-day muckrakers, but by no means are they the only ones. Other journalists, authors, and organizations, sometimes at high personal risk, help to sustain the health of our democracy by "shining light in dark corners." *Vice*, for example, regularly covers tough stories in war zones and other dangerous places. In 2017, *Vice* reporter Elle Reeve spent time with white supremacists preparing to protest the removal of Confederate statues from parks in Charlottesville, Virginia. The next day, a car ran into a crowd of counterprotesters (peaceful protesters expressing their opposition to racism), killing a young demonstrator named Heather Heyer.

Today's muckrakers cover some of the same topics the first muckrakers did. In his book *Fast Food Nation*, for example, Erich Schlosser exposed questionable practices in the production of fast food, the health risks of eating fast food, and the dangerous working conditions for fast-food restaurant employees.

Barbara Ehrenreich, author of *Nickel and Dimed: On (Not) Getting By in America*, exposed the near impossibility of surviving in the United States as a low-wage employee. She did so by going undercover as a waitress, hotel maid, and other service workers.

In October 2017, a muckraking radio program named *Reveal*, which is produced by the Center for Investigative Reporting, aired a story that calls to mind *The Jungle*. It described a trend on the part of judges to send convicts to work

Today's muckrakers include Barbara Ehrenreich, who has drawn attention to the difficulty of surviving on the US minimum wage.

camps instead of jail. These camps claim to help convicts learn a work ethic and beat drug and alcohol addiction. But the work camp featured in the show, which operated a chicken processing plant, did not pay the men any wages at all. As a means of controlling their workers, factory bosses regularly threatened to send the workers back to prison. *Reveal* found evidence the company owners pocketed compensation funds workers won after being injured on the job.

In the days and weeks after the story aired, at least three lawsuits were filed against the work camp, arguing that it violates statutes against forced labor.

assailed," Roosevelt said. Not only will the next story be doubted, but the public will become deadened to actual corruption and injustice, especially if "decent men" are caught in a wide net, he said.

"Too Hot"

Ray Stannard Baker considered the speech a betrayal, and many historians say the speech helped bring about the eventual decline of the muckrakers. Roosevelt did give a "carefully measured" speech that praised the muckrakers as much as it criticized them, says Doris Kearns Goodwin. But in the end, she says, the negative parts got all the attention. "His speech was widely received as an indiscriminate attack on all reform journalists," she wrote in *The Bully Pulpit*.

The *Literary Digest*, a popular magazine of the day, said that the words "man with the muck-rake" were "stamped upon the public mind" after Roosevelt's speech. It quoted the *New York Sun*:

> It was a great day while it lasted, but it became too hot. The Muck-rakers worked merrily for a time in their own bright sunshine, and an unthinking populace applauded their performance. Now there are few to do them reverence.

In a letter to his friend Roosevelt, writer James Brander Matthews made a very accurate prediction. "That is a good piece you spoke about the Man with the Muck-Rake," he said. "And you spoke it at the right moment, so that the name will stick."

Decline of the Muckrakers

There were other factors besides Roosevelt's speech that contributed to the decline of the muckrakers. Some, including Upton Sinclair, claimed there was a conspiracy on the part of business leaders to shut down muckraking magazines. These conspirators supposedly targeted the magazines by getting advertisers to boycott the magazines and banks to refuse to give the magazines loans or to demand that the magazines immediately repay loans they already had. Others say readers simply lost interest, perhaps out of "corruption fatigue."

Perhaps the biggest nail in the coffin was the start of World War I in 1914. Industries and industry leaders were important to the war effort. It would be difficult for reporters to go after them for fraud without seeming to be unpatriotic and turning off readers. In wartime, people often rally behind their government and aren't as open to reading about corruption in government. Likewise, many journalists get assigned to cover the war, so publications have fewer resources for reporting on issues that are not related to the war.

Another important factor in the decline of the muckrakers was the breakup of the muckraking group at *McClure's* magazine. Beginning in 1906, the staff became more and more disenchanted with the brilliant but unpredictable S. S. McClure. When it seemed clear the married publisher had fallen in love with a poet named Florence Wilkinson, they were concerned. If word were to get out that McClure was not faithful to his wife, the magazine—which depended on a spotless reputation, since it was in the business of exposing the wrongdoing of others—would be ruined.

As McClure's unfaithfulness to his wife continued and involved more women, the staff became more troubled. Then, McClure announced he had a major new vision for *McClure's*. He wanted to start a new journal that would reach even more people and have six businesses operating under its umbrella. These businesses would include a bank, a publishing company, a library, and more. The staff thought the plan was grandiose and, in a word, crazy.

With their own professional futures at stake, Tarbell, Steffens, Baker, and other muckrakers left *McClure's* and bought their own magazine, which they named the *American Magazine*. It never succeeded to the extent that *McClure's* had succeeded. It featured muckraking articles while also including more literary stories and lifestyle articles.

Elsewhere, some muckraking magazines were being bought out by publishers who weren't interested in investigative or reform journalism. Other magazines started giving less and less space to long, investigative features. All these factors together helped end the muckraking movement of the Progressive Era.

Legislative Reform

Before their heyday was over, the muckrakers wrote nearly two thousand articles. As we have seen, their reporting led directly or indirectly to important reforms. Upton Sinclair's *The Jungle* and Samuel Hopkins Adams's investigations into patent medicines lead to passage of the Pure Food and Drug Act, which prohibited "the manufacture, sale, or transportation of adulterated or misbranded or poisonous or deleterious foods, drugs or medicines, and liquors." The act also set the stage for eventual creation of the Food and

Drug Administration, which today monitors our food supply, regulates drugs, and issues alerts such as food recalls. *The Jungle* was also an important factor in the passage of the Meat Inspection Act, which required safe production and accurate branding of meat. These two laws marked the beginning of a more active role for government in protecting the people and seeing to their welfare.

Ida Tarbell's investigation of Standard Oil helped lead to the breakup of Standard Oil and set a new standard for careful and thorough citing of facts and painstaking fairness in reporting and analyzing facts. In 1999, New York University's journalism school assembled a panel of leading journalists, historians, and journalism teachers to name the top one hundred works of twentieth-century journalism. Tarbell's was number five.

Number six was Lincoln Steffens's *The Shame of the Cities*, which drew attention to local and state corruption and influenced voters to elect reformers into office instead of the "party faithful." In a similar way, David Phillips's muckraking articles highlighting corruption in the US Senate led to the Seventeenth Amendment.

Jacob Riis's articles and photos helped bring about numerous reforms in New York City, including the Tenement House Act, which required improvements to tenements such as better lighting and ventilation.

Children benefited from the muckraking movement as well. In 1880, there were more than one million children under sixteen working in the United States, which translated to about one in six children. Muckrakers such as John Spargo and Edwin Markham drew attention to these exploited children and helped bring about child labor laws that made it illegal for children under fourteen to work

Some muckrakers worked to protect children in a time before child labor laws. Here, young boys work for a coal mine in 1890.

(farmwork was treated differently) and that set limits on the number of hours children ages fourteen to sixteen could work.

In addition, the muckrakers helped create a new way of thinking about society, its winners and losers, and the role of government. "They turned local issues into national issues, local protests into national crusades. They didn't preach to the converted; they did the converting, helping transform America from a laissez-faire to a welfare state mentality," says historian Jessica Dorman.

Finally, by their example and impact, the muckrakers gave life to the tradition of investigative journalism in the United States and elsewhere.

Woodward and Bernstein

In June 1972, two young reporters barely out of college began reporting on a story that would eventually bring down a presidency. An alert security guard had caught five burglars inside offices of the Democratic National Committee in a Washington, DC, building complex known as Watergate. The burglars had been caught photographing documents and planting eavesdropping devices.

The two *Washington Post* reporters, Carl Bernstein and Bob Woodward, began covering the break-in and trying to determine if there was a connection to people involved with the White House. At first, they were the only reporters working on the story. The White House, under President Richard Nixon, criticized their reporting, insisting the whole affair was nothing more than "a third-rate burglary."

But Woodward and Bernstein kept at it, and they slowly uncovered facts that suggested Nixon's staff members might have known about the break-in or even ordered

The muckrakers paved the way for Watergate reporters Bob Woodward *(left)* and Carl Bernstein (*right*). Their investigation led to Richard Nixon's resignation as US president.

it. They interviewed hundreds of people, many of whom insisted on remaining anonymous. Their editors allowed this but insisted the two reporters had to have more than one source for anonymous facts.

Woodward met at least seventeen times with a highly placed source who would not be quoted but would only confirm facts and suggest new questions to ask. This source became known as "Deep Throat." Very often, he and Woodward met in a garage in Rosslyn, Virginia. Only in 2005 was Deep Throat's identity revealed, when Mark Felt, former assistant director of the FBI, broke his silence in an article in *Vanity Fair* magazine titled "I'm the Guy They Called Deep Throat."

Eventually, the US Senate began its own investigation, during which it became known that President Nixon tape-recorded conversations in the Oval Office. Though Nixon resisted releasing the tapes, the Supreme Court ordered him to. The tapes, which showed Nixon had been involved in a cover-up of the burglary early on (and shocked the nation with the amount of profanity Nixon used), were the final straw. Facing impeachment, Nixon resigned on August 9, 1974. The next president, Gerald Ford, pardoned Nixon so he would not have to go to jail. So far, Nixon is the only American president to have resigned from office.

Woodward and Bernstein became household names. They wrote two best-selling books about Nixon and Watergate, and the better-known of these books, *All the President's Men*, became a major motion picture starring Robert Redford and Dustin Hoffman. The film was a blockbuster that won several Academy Awards.

Many young people were inspired by the tale of two reporters who wouldn't quit and who were willing to take on the most powerful men in the country; journalism school enrollments increased significantly after Watergate. Historian Michael Shudson of the University of California, San Diego, says that Watergate led to "the renewal, reinvigorization and remythologization of muckraking." In the time between the Progressive Era muckrakers and Woodward and Bernstein, there were no famous muckrakers, he says. "But Woodward and Bernstein did not simply renew, they extended the power of the muckraking image," Shudson argues, by tracking corruption all the way to the White House.

Woodward is still an investigative journalist at the *Washington Post*, and since Watergate he has written numerous books about US presidents. Bernstein left the *Post* shortly after Watergate and wrote a variety of investigative articles and books, including books about Pope John Paul II and Hillary Rodham Clinton, former first lady and the first woman to be nominated by a major political party to run for president.

A New Muckraking Era?

Looking at the work of today's journalists, and the strength of today's organizations dedicated to investigative reporting, many people say we are in a new Golden Age of Journalism. Modern muckrakers have an advantage Tarbell, Sinclair, Steffens, Baker, Phillips, Adams, and others did not: the internet. They can pool their efforts more easily, find information with the click of some keys, and even retrieve at their desks the kinds of primary documents that used to require a trip to the library. But these tools are only part of their arsenal. Despite the internet advantage, they are still doing the old-fashioned legwork of which the Progressive Era muckrakers would be proud.

In late 2016 and early 2017, the news media in the United States found itself under attack to an unprecedented degree,

Honors
for Muckrakers

Generally speaking, the muckrakers received more honors and awards posthumously (after death) than as living journalists prone to making trouble for people in power. Today, several have their lives remembered and interpreted by museums and landmarks. There is the Ida B. Wells-Barnett Museum in Mississippi, for example, which includes memorabilia and other Wells artifacts, as well as the Ida B. Wells-Barnett House in Chicago, a National Historic Landmark.

Muckrakers have also been honored on US postage stamps, which

Muckrakers including Ida Wells have had US postage stamps issued in their honor.

Google honored Wells with a Google Doodle in 2015.

throughout the twentieth century was a significant honor. William Allen White (issued in 1948), Wells (1990), Nellie Bly (2002), Ida Tarbell (2002), and Harriet Beecher Stowe (2007) all received commemorative stamps. Like all subjects so honored, they were nominated by an advisory committee for final approval by the postmaster general.

Another popular honor appears in the digital realm: Google Doodles. These special logos on the Google search page honor inventors, artists, scientists, and other pioneers. On July 16, 2015, Google honored Wells with a doodle marking her 153rd birthday, and on May 5, 2015, it honored Bly with a doodle for her 151st birthday.

with repeated statements by President Donald Trump that reporters working for the *New York Times*, CNN, and other mainstream outlets are "enemies of the people." The remarks echoed similar criticism leveled against reporters by Richard Nixon when he was being investigated for his Watergate crimes.

But the mainstream and investigative reporters today don't appear to let the angry words or calculated attacks from the highest office in the land stop them in their work. They know they are not enemies of the people; in fact, they are the opposite. They are a vital part of democracy whose work pushes society to improve and helps the nation to realize its founding ideals. As individuals, most of today's investigative journalists share the feelings Ray Stannard Baker once expressed when he said of the Progressive Era muckrakers: "We were not hopeless, we were not bitter, we were not cynical."

"We 'muckraked,' he said, "not because we hated our world, but because we loved it."

Ray Stannard Baker was a leading muckraker who covered many social issues, including labor movements.

Reporters attend a White House press briefing in December 2017. Today's journalists continue to ask tough questions and tell important stories.

Chronology

1791 The Bill of Rights is ratified. It includes the First Amendment, which guarantees freedom of the press.

1830 The first penny paper is published.

1887 Nellie Bly publishes *Ten Days in a Madhouse*.

1890 Jacob Riis publishes *How the Other Half Lives*.

1892 Ida B. Wells publishes *Southern Horrors: Lynch Law in All Its Phases*.

1893 The first edition of *McClure's* magazine is out at an unheard-of price: fifteen cents per copy.

1899 Edwin Markham publishes his muckraking poem "The Man with a Hoe."

1901 Josiah Flynt publishes *The World of Graft*; New York State passes the Tenement House Act in response to Riis's book.

1902 *McClure's* publishes Lincoln Steffens's article "Tweed Days in St. Louis" and the first of Ida Tarbell's Standard Oil articles.

1903 *McClure's* publishes a January edition many regard as the muckraking movement's start.

1904 Lincoln Steffens publishes *The Shame of the Cities*.

1905 Samuel Hopkins Adams's *The Great American Fraud* exposes dirty-dealing in patent medicine.

1906 Upton Sinclair's *The Jungle*, John Spargo's *The Bitter Cry of Children*, and David Graham Phillips's "The Treason of the Senate" are published; President Theodore Roosevelt describes the crusading journalists as "muckrakers," a label that would stick until today; the Pure Food and Drug Act is passed; the Meat Inspection Act is passed.

1907 Tarbell, Baker, and Steffens leave *McClure's* to found *American Magazine*.

1908 Ray Stannard Baker publishes *Following the Color Line*, instigated by the 1906 Atlanta race riot.

1913 The Seventeenth Amendment passes, which means US senators are now elected by popular vote.

1914 World War I begins; the muckraking movement will subside but has set new standards and approaches for journalism.

1972 Carl Bernstein and Bob Woodward publish a series of articles about the Watergate break-in that will lead President Richard Nixon to resign.

2016 Donald Trump is elected US president and begins regularly attacking journalists as liars and their stories as "fake news." Journalists continue to report.

Glossary

Gilded Age Mark Twain coined this term to describe the decades at the end of the nineteenth century, gleaming and golden on the outside but underneath masking serious social ills, especially poverty.

graft The gaining of wealth through stealing or other illegal means. Muckraker Josiah Flynt, who liked to spend time with hobos and tramps, introduced this term into general usage.

industrialization A shift from a more rural society and economy to a more city-centered, manufacturing-oriented one.

laissez-faire A belief that government should not interfere in the workings of business.

monopoly A company with near-total or total control over an industry that blocks out competition.

muckrakers Journalists writing at the turn of the twentieth century who exposed problems that resulted from rapid urbanization and industrialization. These problems included poverty, disease, exploitation of workers and immigrants, child labor, and more.

party machines Political organizations such as the famous Tammany Hall in New York City that at the turn of the nineteenth century controlled many aspects of city life and government and were corrupt.

penny papers Newspapers that sold for one cent beginning in the 1800s. They revolutionized journalism because they greatly expanded newspapers' readership.

Progressive Reform Era/Progressive Era A period of intense activism and reform, roughly from the 1890s until the 1920s.

progressive reformers People including reporters, politicians, workers, and activists who pushed for social reforms during the Progressive Reform Era.

ragpickers People, often Italian immigrants, who made a living picking rags and bones up in the street and selling them.

robber barons Industrial tycoons, such as John D. Rockefeller, who became tremendously wealthy during the Gilded Age, often through unethical or unscrupulous means.

socialism A different economic system than that of the United States, which employs capitalism. In a socialist system, more of the wealth is controlled by everyone, and services such as health care and education are available to all and paid for by taxes. During the Progressive Era, some people argued for socialism as a fairer system, but others, such as Theodore Roosevelt, thought that was naïve.

tenements Apartment buildings. During the Progressive Era, tenements in large cities were overcrowded, disease-ridden, and dirty.

tramps Unemployed men who traveled the country looking either for work or a handout. Called tramps because they "tramped" all over the country. The term became synonymous with "hobo."

transcontinental railroads The first railroads to join the eastern and western parts of the United States.

urbanization When an area becomes a city.

yellow journalism A form of journalism that relied on dramatic and often exaggerated presentation of news, designed to sell newspapers.

Further Information

Books

Bodden, Valerie. *The Muckrakers: Ida Tarbell Takes on Big Business*. North Mankato, MN: ABDO Publishing, 2017.

Hillstrom, Laurie Collier. *The Muckrakers and the Progressive Era*. Detroit, MI: Omnigraphics, 2010.

Marrin, Albert. *The Great Adventure: Theodore Roosevelt and the Rise of Modern America*. New York: Dutton Children's Books, 2007.

Yochelson, Bonnie. *Jacob A. Riis: Revealing New York's Other Half: A Complete Catalogue of His Photographs*. New Haven, CT: Yale University Press, 2015.

Websites

America on the Move: Community Dreams

http://americanhistory.si.edu/america-move/community-dreams

Learn more about how railroads fit into the larger picture of industrialization and why Frank Norris wrote the muckraking classic *The Octopus*.

Ray Stannard Baker Articles

http://www.historicjournalism.com/ray-stannard-baker.html

Read a selection of Baker's articles, including "The Right to Work."

Upton Sinclair's End Poverty in California Campaign

http://depts.washington.edu/epic34/

Learn more about Sinclair's fight to end poverty on this comprehensive website hosted by the University of Washington.

The Woodward and Bernstein Watergate Papers

http://www.hrc.utexas.edu/exhibitions/web/woodstein

The University of Texas at Austin paid $5 million to acquire the notes and other papers of Woodward and Bernstein. Now you can browse the cache on the UT website.

Videos

C-SPAN Cities Tour - Erie: Ida Tarbell Papers
https://www.youtube.com/watch?v=KSskKr4a95E

Professor Paula Treckel presents information about Ida Tarbell and *The History of the Standard Oil Company*.

How We Got to Now with Steven Johnson: Jacob Riis PBS
https://www.youtube.com/watch?v=VFaPy2Ye0kU

See the (explosive) flash technology used by Riis in action.

Lower East Side Tenement Museum
https://www.youtube.com/watch?v=KNqe6QA7cYM

Explore the museum's offerings and hear about its unique history.

Bibliography

Adams, Samuel Hopkins. *The Great American Fraud.*
Reprinted from *Collier's* Weekly. Retrieved November
28, 2017. http://www.gutenberg.org/files/44325/44325-
h/44325-h.htm.

Baker, Ray Stannard. *Following the Color Line: An Account of
Negro Citizenship in the American Democracy.* New York:
Doubleday, Page & Company, 1908.

Burns, Ric. *New York: A Documentary Film.* Directed by Ric
Burns. 1999.

Chalmers, David Mark. *The Social and Political Ideas of
Muckrakers.* New York: Citadel Press, 1964.

Conwell, Russell H. *Acres of Diamonds.* Philadelphia: Temple
University Press, 2002.

Dorman, Jessica. "Where Are Muckraking Journalists Today?"
Nieman Reports, June 15, 2000. http://niemanreports.
org/articles/where-are-muckraking-journalists-today.

Filler, Louis. *Crusaders for American Liberalism: The Story of
the Muckrakers.* Yellow Springs, OH: Antioch College
Press, 1950.

Goodwin, Doris Kearns. *The Bully Pulpit: Theodore Roosevelt, William Howard Taft, and the Golden Age of Journalism.* New York: Simon & Schuster, 2013.

Harriet Beecher Stowe Center. "Life: Harriet Beecher Stowe." Retrieved November 28, 2017. https://www.harrietbeecherstowecenter.org.

History of American Journalism. "A History of American Journalism in the 20th Century." Retrieved November 28, 2017. http://history.journalism.ku.edu.

Miraldi, Robert, ed. *The Muckrakers: Evangelical Crusaders.* Westport, CT: Praeger Publishers, 2000.

National Park Service. "Jacob Riis Biography." Last updated February 26, 2015. https://www.nps.gov/gate/learn/historyculture/jacob-riis-biography.htm.

Quirk, Tom, and Gary Scharnhorst, eds. *American History Through Literature 1870–1920.* New York: Charles Scribner's Sons, 2006.

Riis, Jacob. *How The Other Half Lives: Studies Among the Tenements of New York*. Eastford, CT: Martino Fine Books, 2015.

Sinclair, Upton. *The Autobiography of Upton Sinclair*. New York: Harcourt, Brace, & World, Inc., 1962.

———. *The Jungle*. Mineola, NY: Dover Publications, 2001.

Stowe, Harriet Beecher. *Uncle Tom's Cabin*. Seattle, WA: AmazonClassics, 2017.

Tarbell, Ida. *The History of the Standard Oil Company*. Mineola, NY: Dover Publications, 2003.

Woodward, Bob, and Carl Bernstein. *All the President's Men*. New York: Simon & Schuster, 1974.

Young, James Harvey. *The Toadstool Millionaires*. Princeton, NJ: Princeton University Press, 1972.

Index

Page numbers in **boldface** are illustrations.

About the Author

Jacqueline Conciatore Senter has written extensively about media and is the author of *Peaceful Protesters: Martin Luther King Jr.: Fulfilling a Dream.* She lives with her husband, Michael, in Fairfax, Virginia.